LOVE

with

POSITIVE ENERGY

TAHA MOHAMED BENNIS

MILTON & HUGO L.L.C.
4407 Park Ave., Suite 5
Union City, NJ 07087, USA

Website: *www. miltonandhugo.com*
Hotline: *1- 888-778-0033*
Email: *info@miltonandhugo.com*

Ordering Information:
Quantity sales. Special discounts are available on quantity purchases by corporations, associations, and others. For details, contact the publisher at the address above.

Library of Congress Control Number: 2024907529
ISBN-13:   979-8-89285-083-4   [Paperback Edition]
                  979-8-89285-082-7   [Digital Edition]

Rev. date: 03/25/2024

No judgement for the actions.

As a desire is hard to achieve.

The experience with hardship for the pride that comes as a relief.

No matter what no one could prevent the person's dream.

As a personality becomes the service for the market needs.

For the procedures it has the characteristics.

As a rule to follow for the interest with the love and critics.

The knowledge with the passion of the statistics.

As a mixture could create lessons with the blessings.

The kindness is a coefficient for organization and success.

To motivate as a role model to spread the reputation for the companions.

As the beauty is so positive that comes with the education that improves inspiration.

The scientist figures out the negatives to beware for all the attention.

As the grace is available while the growth start to admit.

The beginning of being grateful while the talent is about to prosper from the spirit.

The mentality as a source with acceptance of the belief that could sparkle.

Even if it doesn't come perfect it stills an effort trial from the heart.

God in trust with freedom as every citizen are benevolent.

Everyone can exchange thought as a merciful that gives a chance more than a limit.

As a powerful country that confesses about the worldwide harmony.

Understanding the logic while everyone are in their row for happiness.

As this lovely writing could be a wish.

It changes and flips a lot as a wave that everytime has an event.

To challenge from resources to produce a benefit.

With the best effort as a release guidance posted public.

The learning from the mistakes that master the deeds as another top.

As a cover from the past that keeps memories to improvise so easily.

The Poet Taha Mohamed Bennis.

When the life doesn't give me anything.

As between the earth and the sky.

The creation as an engine.

Not exceeding the limit.

But the logic is something right.

Looking at the beauty for reasons.

So beautiful as it is empty.

Filling out with meaning of creativity.

To prove as I am a good guy.

Nothing could be hidden.

As a lie could turn to the truth.

At the time would be demonstrated.

Figuring out with the hard work.
And never give up.

The beauty is everywhere.
As the sun start to shine for the result.

By many deeds with themes.
And the science with mentality.

Even life doesn't give anything.
We think about it to enjoy it.

As many solutions started.

when the dark comes to the light.

As to promote for the success.

Humble and a good guy.

I will never abandon all the satisfaction.

The love always wins.

And kindness always has a meaning.

The achievement would never fade.

And the best moments for the rest of the heaven.

The poet Taha Mohamed Bennis.

Dancing with the melody and having fun.

Following the rhymes as enjoying the sound.

As the feelings as the amazing talent

Moving around for the best entertainment.

As the music going backward and forward.

To make as a distance and so manageable.

The life as the example and the message.

To deliver the meaning as an art of the intelligence.

The love would never fade.

Even the hate and the mean.

It still exist as an enemy.

However not to destroy as killing and fighting.

The education is always at the top.

To understand between a word and against it

As the collection from the level of the rates

With the reception of all the satisfaction.

With the availability of the security and the justice.

As the majority and minority are compromised.

To see the usual and unusual performance.

With the lovely respect as a unity.

The powerful themes as the wonderful artists.

The excitement from beating the heat.

And getting finally the air as the relief.

Fresh and clean as lovely the end of the sacrifice deeds.

The way from the creator and the creation.

From the grace to the enjoyment.

Even the love can be addicted.

As a positive way to be so nice and educated.

As the life is so beautiful with the thought of it

the luckiest and the smartest find the treasure in it.

So deep as expressive and meaningful.

The guidance to love the beauty and to attract for the potential.

As an interest of the future champion.

The best effort no matter what in process.

As the reputation spread in the worldwide.

The art is very an amazing talent from the source of the heart

The poet Taha Mohamed bennis.

Hip hop.

The knowledge with the rules and the clock.

As time flies with the basics to be smart.

Everything is demonstrated as an easy challenge.

For every source and mentality to check what it got.

From the dreams to reality it might be hard.

For the effort to make a lovely one.

The adventure is like a wise art.

The best made is the wonderful master from the heart.

With the loyalty is the one to create the love with the trust.

Intelligence is the cling to get stuck in it.

With good deeds to show up the sweat.

For the energy is to produce as a benefit.

For every difference to make it as it fits.

From the grace of God to enjoyment.

The exploit from the chance to be a master.

With a lot of pieces could gather as simple.

And the admires come with the blessings.

From the history to the poetry.

It might be a pretend to feel how to try it.

The journalist is with the person who loves everyone.

As the interest will be shared as posted in public.

The poet Taha Mohamed Bennis.

Marrakech.

The love would never fade.

But the beauty is always the same.

From history to the present.

Everyone are here for the development.

With many challenges to attract and to bring.

The lovely grace that saves the community as attractiveness.

Joking a lot and making the happiest day.

The most powerful as it is and never changes.

As the building is embellished with intelligence of art.

Many creative artists try to show love with good deeds as benevolence.

Everyday is a better day.

Enjoy the comfort with the sunrise until it sets.

With a warm welcome as good weather is so suitable as the happiness.

With the melody comes around as impressive.

The world would recognize more as the opportunity of relaxing.

With the education so addicted as the top educated and healthy.

So nice and clean and it is an appreciation to everybody.

The poet Taha Mohamed bennis.

The rich man deeds might look like a diamond.

Cause of the fateness of God and the magic.

A hero man might show up the manhood of the struggle from the heart and the muscle.

Cause of the man we might love the confidence, but they receive the tenderness and fight against the corruption.

And for all rights, is the respect of ladies and gentlemen.

And the poor with the needs, we might share and spread to the neighborhoods.

And cause of the love and a good reputation.

Feel by the person feelings and taking care by raising donations.

And we might love with a pleasure way with modestly heart.

And with no problem, there is always the attraction and the benefits of this life.

Cause for the blessings and the recycle there is no wasting time.

The poet Taha Mohamed Bennis.

The good guy

Amazing guy…

The love as a harmony.

Creating the art as a beauty.

Making something true for the loyalty.

It never ends even it fades.

No surrender for its value and the time.

Having fun and enjoying the life.

With the deeds and the help we all need.

Being strong and nice for the community.

As the attention of the majority.

We love to create for every victory.

So powerful but going upward and downward.

As the wind going forward and backward.

And with the recover of any direction.

For solving the problems and make it smartest.

With the lesson and the blessings.

We love to take care as the good emotions.

As the harmony is very important.

Cause the priority of the safety make us worry.

God almighty is present.

And the reward of consistently is the hope.

Encouragement is a better way to describe.

To improve the happiness and to memorize.

The application of the passion desire.

We can do everything as a better life.

Poet Taha Mohamed Bennis.

The Loveliest Hiba.

Ali finally just found his love.

To express his favorite with the favor.

With kindness and many flavors.

He chooses from his heart as the most important.

Ali can do anything to make you the happiest.

Your smile give him energy as the luckiest.

He keeps looking around and found out you are so special. While he is very nice and humble.

Your man is so strong than you ever carry a fashion model.

The loveliest he can imagine since he met you

To celebrate the history together as peace and to enjoy.

As the mystery coming to take care to each other.

With the satisfaction and the compromise.

The best can equally sacrifice for the love and keep strong together.

Having fun like an angel and feeding the birds like a sweet valentine.

Love always wins no matter what.

With the deeds comes from the words as the wonderful confidence.

As the gentleman Ali would love to build steps as the future generations.

And the hope to stay longer with happiness and joy.

To prosper the land as Ali and Hiba are walking for an excursion.

To be proud from the moment to the certificate.

The confirmation is an amazing love that will keep always forward and forever.

The poet Taha Mohamed Bennis.

The blessings.

The love with many activities.

Step by step until the reach of the victory.

It takes time to prosper the favor with honestly deeds.

It get used that will become a memory of no anxiety.

The happiness is the enjoyment to be a good person.

Dealing with everyone as the same treatment of love.

Doesn't matter if it is depressed from the evil.

The activeness is the example to fight against with application.

And even it comes as a profit.

The attitude never change with much pleasing of guidance.

That give feelings with the appreciation of caring more.

Without ignorance that server could get paid as a savior.

To strength the idiom for the experience to live as a native with admiration.

Even the thought is the best from source of imagination.

The fact would never change that everyone should understand it.

As a rhetorical mind will give a didactic to express with many ways.

The solutions comes to manage between anger and kindness.

As the creativity deserve much better attention.

The forgiveness is a lot granted for at least to admit.

After the satisfaction the angels pray for the benevolent as a praise from the education.

The poet Taha Mohamed Bennis

Is not about your beauty.

Is about the deeds that match your creativity.

Even the enemy try to interfere as a prudent.

You are wiser to know the advantage rather than a surrender and be his sinister.

As long you are the happiest darling.

I might deliver the message with so much love as an amazing person.

While the personality is accompanied with you as a whole brand reputation.

You know who is your worth as a savior, prince charming, and you are the survivor.

The modesty heart would love to take care of you.

As the praise that one action could cover the rest of you.

As the sharing is to compromise with kindness.

With no worries we are the couples for the blessings.

The message come through as finally we resolve the problem.

The same rights we get when we enjoy the moment of solution.

The relief comes as an art that no one distracts for the envy.

Cause we hide it for the gift of the future.

That we invite further generation from the history impacts.

While the promise would always fight for every reasons.

The ability to live is to think creative about the challenges that you are a treasure.

The fairness that I performed is the result of the merit.

Even it is difficult for everyone.

The success from the determination match the assistance from the satisfaction.

The poet Taha Mohamed Bennis.

Rewind everything to the wind.

It will come backward and manage the future swing.

The possibilities from the effort can show up to bring.

To amaze from the attractiveness won't be regretted.

As the decision comes to every right.

Every ideas is with no limit that has the way without escape.

That adds the enjoyment plus the security is equal the law of justice.

The time flies while the hope is always around the sky.

No matter what God is always touching the heart with a lot of fear and goosebumps.

The beauty is from the creator that make the Excellence.

As the nation could embellish or damage it.

While with favor and the service is always protected.

As the mood changes all the time.

The emotions could not control the faith from the effects.

Even the love could be addictive.

The evil and welfare are together for the adventure.

Never give up for the livelihood.

The knowledge should be granted from the first generation book.

That spreads until they improve from many trials as it forwards.

To the almighty who sees and make it appreciated.

Cause everything is for reasons.

The same as the examples from the way it logics.

The tool for the use that kind of wisdom.

It shows up everyone as the angel and challenges the deeds as freedom.

What a lovely blessings.

The nature is absolutely right and straight.

Nothing is missed from the lies and the gossips.

Everything is demonstrated to exploit.

To extract the beauty to the deals.

That if they violate it comes the results of disasters and nightmares.

And that how life is since we born to be alive until the day of judgements.

The poet Taha Mohamed Bennis.

The addiction of a lot of thought.

Many ideas come with certainty and doubt.

From the heart is not demonstrated the most.

In life needs to provide sacrifice even if it's difficult.

As an adventure is to fight against the obstacles.

The deeds are so strong that will never give up.

The creator grants to harmony different ways to figure out.

To produce a good energy to prove the love of God in trust.

No matter what the news says as given reports.

The belief keeps always positive as kind and smart.

The guidance turns into goosebumps and

fear to the greatest.

A didactic way to represent the beauty as a memory art.

The poet taha Mohamed Bennis.

I am an artist in your dreams.

As a wish to see me the best humble.

Working hard for the satisfactory.

I collect the worldwide love as a mystery.

The future are waiting for me to be present.

The hope as a beauty everyday I fight.

Against the obstacles that has a blessing and a lesson.

By the grace of God to the enjoyment.

I am good guy for peace with the lovely moment.

The best I can perform to the market.

They can remind me of my experiences.

I will never abandon the love.

To figure out everyone minds as a science.

The heart will touch as a humanity.

I choose the kindness that keeps so united.

That I am a good guy with the determination.

I say that I will do it.

For the success that I will accomplish it.

No matter what I always grow up.

For the effort that I will appreciate it.

Until I master the wonderful deeds.

I will thank as a mercy who let me do it.

Until I benefit the love with values.

With the respect and the salute.

I prefer everyone as the same treat.

To have their own profession for always to the needs.

The stress I felt.

Looking around as deep as I want to correct.

To manage between right and left.

I become so smart that I found the perfect.

As she just greets.

The beautiful eyes cannot miss.

So innocent and sweet.

The reasons that come with love always wins.

And I recite to admit.

I confront her with the brave and not timid.

The source of the heart would never deny me

As the promise is the freedom that won't lie to me.

To grow as the richest we can reach.

The hope is waiting for us as a gift.

Even the hate and mean exist.

We control it with the deeds that we are together with.

With the surprise that I can grant.

To share my intelligence as a lovely prudent.

As the lovely chance that was fated.

I mean by complement and not advertisement.

The secret give us the reason of compromise.

And finally we spread the truth that we are along forever.

The poet Taha Mohamed Bennis.

The deeds can bring everything.

The loyalty as pleasant.

The energy is by the love and not to exploit.

Even as a good opportunity has been granted.

The joy is to accept anything for the favor.

As the service is a pleasure to meet.

From everywhere that manages it's own greet.

The happiness from passion that is seen as it fits.

The more longer stays is a member for benefits.

The cling with admiration will get its' results.

The habit as a sensitive feeling is excited for the potential.

The expression with deep words that creates an art.

Not the craziness but is the practice that gets so successful.

As the deeds can bring everything.

The fate that it gathers the blessing.

Learning from the experience that comes with desires.

A lot of satisfaction will be the major on person's mind.

As from the modest with much support.

The value grows with more welcome.

Nothing is easy and for free.

That makes a hard lesson with good sacrifice.

Many appreciation and opinions.

That is a cause for social culture with a salutation.

With the knowledge as a science that attracts.

Everyone could be a champion no matter what.

Even is not perfect.

Is still loved from source of the heart.

Everyone needs but is with the patience.

The people's rights are in the row that no one is deprived at all.

The poet Taha Mohamed Bennis.

My mum said by her spirit from the sky.

I am a good guy but I still have some issues
incompetent.

I said I am struggling and doing my best because is the
way to obey and being modest.

She worried everytime about me while she is on the
heaven.

But thank God she is really alive without knocking the
door from the families and is all her convenient.

I love God and I love everybody.

But my heart feels so hesitant because I still wonder for the forgiveness.

But one day I pray God and supplicate.

Whatever bad treatment I feel.

I know that the justice is in the hereafter and not the police.

And henceforward that my dream is to get up from the sleep and work more harder than I think.

And make everyone the most happiest about me.

Cause I am a good guy.

And for the welfare and the goodwill.

I make the future for myself, but everybody love the interest about me.

They want me to succeed and see me the best wonderful guy I ever achieve.

The poet Taha Mohamed Bennis.

The love would never hesitate.

To inspire that it addresses the truth.

He would finally love to confront.

To say that she has a lovely heart.

The sunshine comes as a smile.

Watching the beauty many times.

The deeds come together so nice

The moment that they can enjoy their lives.

As the dark night finally comes.

The silence to relax and for freedom.

The sacrifice end to sleep peaceful.

To produce as a better energy to overcome.

For the best future that make them forward.

To make everyone happy and so proud.

With the satisfaction and the grace of God.

They are a perfect match to each other.

The poet Taha Mohamed Bennis.

The deeds of the sacrifice are demonstrated.

By the heart is the person's experience.

The fight for the obstacle is a good explanation.

By representing the personality in a deep feeling and so creative.

By many projects prosper with the hope.

The ideas is about to fulfill the intention.

By many wishes is the coming of the happiness.

The relief from the worker educated is creating the justice with kindness.

The lovely such as the generations are.

The continuation of the path and the goals to improve forward.

The pride who starts and the companions who follow.

To thank as a high level who invent the key symbols.

To ease and make all the possibilities available for the market.

With different abilities and thinking from the grace of God as so grateful.

The poet Taha Mohamed Bennis.

What a lovely angel.

You grow up with blessings and we hide you the devil.

Always loving you and protect you in order to give you the power of tenderness and the struggle you can provide by fateness of God and the best luck of the splendid future .

God gives a grace and we will make you in the first heart with much more priority and no less.

You will grow up

You will find the beauty inside and outside of you darling.

You will be so beautiful with much more cloths and accessories with shopping.

And with the humblest you will be in a very good education with an amazing parents.

It might grow up the love until you will be so loved.

The poet Taha Mohamed Bennis.

Just look at the girl while she is smiling.

It is a reference to show the appreciation and free welcoming.

Well this is her sweet home, she might feel like a princess and need someone to love.

Gather the families and more for the best caring and support.

With the best of the education would come from her attitude and the culture.

The best lucky man might find this beauty.

Make her a queen, so the man be the lucky king.

The queen of the beauty and the king of everything.

Be always worthed but not crazy about the money!

Cause with the hope and faith.

She might deserve a wonderful world might describe a man.

Humble experiences with the strongest results.

The poet Taha Mohamed Bennis.

They said I am not at the top.

But with the fateness of God.

I leave it discreet until everyone see the change of the wonder reaction.

I collect some love and the satisfaction of the world and the culture understanding splendid logic.

That everyone will celebrate the history, and they will turn as a fated person who love God and love everybody.

Cause I am doing my best with my brain and my muscle.

The way I use I am ready to produce.

With my energy I use, it might be worthed but not wasted.

And even wasted, I might sacrifice again kindly and nicely 'as well not widely as a savage aggressive.

And with the best environment would love to let it protected until everyone see the dreams so close and have fun with the best friends and the loved ones.

Cause I love to help, and God help me by reaching the peace and the best enjoyment.

I find the grace by doing the good things.

Because I know I might be doing like an economy.

But always in progress with failling and the recovery.

And it will be sooner with the big investment future.

That I might take care.

With the happiness and no anger.

That every step we want even would not be in our dreams.

It might be a disaster.

Cause we might use the love and the fateness.

Leave it fated and appreciated.

It gives me the lesson to struggle with the best and the moment of the modest.

I might be a hero.

With the intention of the key success.

Never leave it and God bless.

Poet Taha Mohamed Bennis.

Just look at my math.

Dancing with the music and enjoying like a splash.

I am a good guy who love everyone with the warm welcoming and attracting the worldwide to recognize the new activity as a luminous flash.

Doing my best that all brands use my name as I am an amazing guy with the strongest deeds and speech from the source of my heart.

Splendid careers using for the light with the right personality with description of my charisma.

Art is a logic smart that make money by tickets and with all fun.

Attract as a beginner and let the harmony get used all the way to improvise the improvement.

Laughing for the funniest.

Relaxing for the entertainment.

That my skills is moving that make everyone overthink.

Take advantage for the benefits and work hard for the production.

Success might come by the intention and the morals.

The belief of the invention and to master it from the grace of God almighty to the investment.

Come back as a memory and take care of others that would never forget from the depression.

The modest is important while I figure out the service is a relation of every concept to a survival plus a protection.

Speak up high and never give up for the hope that every condition will be a better moment.

My ideas is squeezing, however it is absolutely coming the result of the excitement.

That life is supposed to be delivered with limited right but not under - privileged and tortured.

Providing the assistance and testimony over me for the certificate with the own expertise solution.

That we use the love and whatever I did that really worth many kindness and blessings and long live the appreciation.

God bless me and bless everybody.

Poet Taha Mohamed Bennis

Milton Keynes UK
Ingram Content Group UK Ltd.
UKHW011911060524
442290UK00001B/154

9 798892 850834